Praise for Daily Calm

'Padraig is extremely ... ...ad and his knowledge of the subject of mindfulness is vast. He has a great ability to explain concepts in simple terms. This book will be a valuable addition to my own practice, and to my work as a psychologist in elite sport.'
Dr Kate Kirby, Olympic sport psychologist and Head of Psychology, Sport Ireland Institute

'A plethora of practical and ingenious insights to help the most stressed amongst us to embrace the rewards of feeling calm. If you want to lead a calmer life, this book is for you. A very clever concept packed full of mindful solutions to help you cultivate inner tranquility in a chaotic world.'
Fiona Brennan, author of *Irish Times* bestseller, *The Positive Habit*

'We need little moments and skills that can bring us from a state of overwhelm to one of calm, courageousness and compassion now, more than ever. *Daily Calm* will give you such moments and skills in simple, accessible, easily digestible chunks in a few short minutes per day. The practices within this book could change the trajectory of your day, and indeed your life when practised consistently over time.'
Aisling Leonard-Curtin, chartered psychologist, co-author of No. 1 *Irish Times* bestseller, *The Power of Small*, and Acceptance and Commitment Therapy Trainer

To the many thousands of readers of the Daily Bell.
This book exists because of you.

About the author

Padraig O'Morain has been practising mindfulness for three decades. He has introduced thousands of people to this life-enhancing practice through his training courses, and his aim is to make it easy and accessible for all. His books have been published in many countries and languages and have brought his approach to readers all over the world. They include *Kindfulness, Mindfulness on the Go, Mindfulness for Worriers* and *Light Mind.* Padraig writes a weekly column for the *Irish Times.* He is also the author of a poetry collection, *The Blue Guitar* (theblueguitar.net). He lives in Dublin with his wife.

Daily Calm

100 daily reminders to help you
build the mindfulness habit

Padraig O'Morain

First published in Great Britain in 2019 by Yellow Kite
An imprint of Hodder & Stoughton
An Hachette UK company

1

Copyright © Padraig O'Morain 2019
Illustrations © May van Millingen

A CIP catalogue record for this title is available from the British Library

Trade Paperback ISBN 978 1 529 31300 0
eBook ISBN 978 1 529 31598 1

Typeset in Celeste 10.5/14 pt by Palimpsest Book Production Limited,
Falkirk, Stirlingshire

Printed and bound in Great Britain by Clays Ltd, Elcograf S.p.A.

Hodder & Stoughton policy is to use papers that are natural, renewable
and recyclable products and made from wood grown in sustainable forests.
The logging and manufacturing processes are expected to conform to
the environmental regulations of the country of origin.

Yellow Kite
Hodder & Stoughton Ltd
Carmelite House
50 Victoria Embankment
London EC4Y 0DZ

www.yellowkitebooks.co.uk

Contents

Introduction

'Mindfulness does not change reality directly, but it does change your relationship with it. And in doing that, it changes everything.'

Padraig O'Morain,
Mindfulness on the Go

Mindfulness means returning your awareness to the present moment, while accepting the reality of your experience in that moment. This simple practice has enhanced – sometimes transformed – the experience of people throughout the world for millennia.

The modern world is busy and more overwhelming than ever, which is why mindfulness is crucial in order to feel calm and cultivate happiness in your daily life. That is why today you will find mindfulness practised in every field you can think of – in business, sports, hospitals, schools and in the home.

It isn't hard to do. To be mindful, you return your awareness frequently to what your senses bring you – to something you see, hear, taste, touch or smell, to awareness of your overall physical sensations. In a way, you become a friendly witness to your own experience as it is happening.

In return, you become calmer, you find it easier to navigate the challenges of your life, you get better at enjoying its pleasures and I think it is generally true that your relationships improve. And there's more: mindfulness helps you to reduce your levels of stress, to recover from stress more quickly, to gain a sense of space in your mind and to enjoy the greater calm that flows from the practice of acceptance.

People sometimes shy away from mindfulness because they think they will have to spend twenty or thirty minutes a day observing their breathing and they are just not ready to do that;

or they think they can't practise mindfulness because they are not spiritual; or they are rushing in the morning and tired in the evening and they fear that they won't have the time or energy for it. But mindfulness is for everybody, not only for spiritual people – and indeed, many who practise mindfulness, including the author of this book, do not see themselves as spiritual. Mindfulness can be practised in short and simple ways and this book will give you many, many ideas as to how to do that.

Moreover, mindfulness is an attitude as well as an exercise – an attitude that sees the experience of ordinary moments as valuable, that encourages acceptance of those experiences we must accept (or that are not worth fighting with) and a sense of well-wishing towards ourselves and others.

This book helps you to cultivate that attitude by gently motivating you to practise a mindfulness exercise at least once a day, however demanding or busy that day may be.

Daily Calm is inspired by, and based on, the 'Daily Bell', a daily reminder to be mindful, which I began to send to a handful of interested people some years ago, unsure if it would gain a following. Today, many thousands of people all over the world receive it and have made it an integral part of their day, in good times and in bad. I hope it will help you to make mindfulness with its many benefits a constant presence in your life. You can subscribe to the Daily Bell, free of charge, at www.padraigomorain.com.

• *How to use this book*

Daily Calm is your everyday companion. Each page focuses on an idea drawn from the philosophy and practice of mindfulness that you can bring into your day, and it suggests ways in which to put the concept into practice. Once you've reached the end of the book, you will find some practices listed under themes, reflecting issues that may arise for you from time to time.

In the Appendix, you will find instructions for a seven-stage mindfulness walk during which you can repeat or contemplate some of your favourite ideas from the book. I developed this walk during a time of stress some years ago and I have been using it ever since; I hope you will try it out (you can also do it in your imagination if you don't feel like putting on your walking shoes or if it's the middle of the night and you're lying awake in bed).

THE LABYRINTH: at the bottom of each page you will find a suggested number directing you to an additional page to look at if you wish. Labyrinths, or mazes, have been used in many cultures for thousands of years for meditation. The concept of a labyrinth as a path along which you can move without knowing what is around the next corner, or where this or that choice will lead you, has made it attractive for reflection.

In this book, you won't know where the 'labyrinth' page number will lead you until you follow it. Sometimes it will outline a further aspect of the subject on the page you came from. Sometimes – and this is deliberate – there will be no obvious link, the aim being to bring a new idea or insight to mind, which can be really helpful. You don't have to follow the labyrinth – it's an extra option if you feel you would like something further – but why not give it a go on days when you have the time to do so and see where it leads you?

1 *Are you worth a moment?*

· · · · · · ·

Are you worth a moment of your own time? Can you allow yourself to just 'be' for a while, perhaps letting yourself enjoy the sensation of breathing?

Sometimes we allow ourselves to be pulled in all directions by the demands of others or of situations because we feel more 'justified' that way. But why should you go through life without ever taking a moment for yourself or feeling bad if you do, as though you're caught in the middle of a tug of war? It's import-ant to be a friend to yourself as well as to others, and that can mean taking time out to simply 'be'.

● *Practice*
Connect with awareness of your breath several times a day: morning, mid-morning, lunchtime, mid-afternoon, evening, before sleep, perhaps. By insisting on doing this, by finding that time (sometimes you have to search even for such little spaces in the day), you affirm that you deserve that mindful moment.

2 *Not a game of chess*

. . . .

Life is not a game of chess. You don't have to spend all your time figuring out moves in your head or worrying about the future. See what awareness of the present moment has to offer instead.

We are problem solvers, but we take it too far. If we find ourselves at rest, at a loose end, we flip into problem-solving mode. Why not say instead: here is a moment in which I don't actually have to solve any problems; and appreciate that? Too often, we walk around, heads down, solving problems in an imaginary future, while completely failing to see what is around us in this moment that we could appreciate.

● *Practice*

Resolve that for half an hour or an hour a day you will not solve any problems in your life. You will simply spend your time being aware of what's going on in the moment. Perhaps try it after you leave work – enjoy your leisure time without continuing to work in your head.

3 Be your own friend, no matter what

• • • • • • •

Can you pledge to be your own friend at the end of the day, whatever happens? Even if you make a mess of things; even if other people criticise you?

Sometimes we're afraid of challenges because we fear how we will attack ourselves if we fail. Often though, the condemnation of ourselves *by* ourselves is tougher than criticism from others. But even if we are harshly criticised by others, we don't have to join in by giving ourselves a kicking. Instead, we can, in a spirit of self-compassion, look at what we might need to change, and change it.

• *Practice*
When you get up each morning, make a silent pledge to yourself that you will still be your own friend at the end of the day, whatever it may bring. That 'whatever' may include success or suffering or both. But know that you can rely on your own friendship, no matter what. If you like affirmations, use the phrase 'True friend' through the day.

4 *Take a breath*

· · · · · · ·

Awareness of breathing takes you straight back to the moment. Instead of just saying, 'I will be mindful of my breathing', try to be specific by choosing one or two practices from the list below or by using another breathing practice you like. Breathing also has physiological and emotional effects – for instance, taking five or six out-breaths engages the part of your nervous system that calms you down. If you dislike breathing exercises, you can choose from the many other methods in this book.

• *Practices*

Out-breath: bring your awareness to your out-breath, watching it gently flow all the way out.

In-breath: rest awareness on your in-breath, observing it happening all by itself.

Count the breaths: the first in-breath and out-breath is one, the second, two and so on, up to seven. Come back to one and start again.

The breath in your nose: bring your attention for a while to the feeling of the breath in your nose.

Visualise: imagine you're standing on the beach. Little wavelets come in slowly, touch your toes and go out again. Coordinate the water coming in with your in-breath and the water going out with your out-breath.

5/9: count to five while you are taking an in-breath and to nine while taking an out-breath.

5 *Give yourself some space*

Many people who practise mindfulness say it gives them a
sense of 'spaciousness' in a busy day. That space between us and
the swirl of events and thoughts brings a sense of calm.

Why should awareness of your breath or posture give you a
sense of space? Probably because in choosing to be mindful, in
a sense, we take charge of how we experience what's happening
to us. We can't take charge of the whole experience – other
people may be involved too. However, we take charge of enough
of it to say, 'I am here too', and to gain a greater sense of awareness.

• Practice
Practise bringing awareness to the breath in your nose and to the
sensations you feel there. This can make you more aware and self-
collected – as you walk down a crowded street full of Friday-evening
shoppers, for instance. Apart from awareness of breathing, all
mindfulness practices help you to experience that sense of
spaciousness.

6 *Mindful moments make a better day*

. . . .

Whatever the content of your day may be, the practice of mindfulness can get you to the end of it in better shape. It means, among other things, staying out of the dramatic stories your mind generates and returning your awareness to this moment.

Practising mindfulness doesn't mean you will float through every day on a sea of calm. Most of us live in circumstances – work or family – that guarantee spikes of stress. And when we talk to ourselves in an exaggerated, repetitive way about what's happening, we prolong that stress. Mindfulness, on the other hand, avoids ramping up the level of stress and allows it to subside more quickly.

• *Practice*
Make a habit of building mindful moments into your day. Think of a simple mindfulness practice, perhaps listening to sounds in the air around you. Work out when you will repeat this during the day – say, morning, lunchtime, evening. Added together, your mindful moments could make a great difference to your emotional wellbeing.

7 Anxious about being anxious?

· · · · · · ·

Anxiety comes with being alive. We need to accept this fact, and we can help ourselves by asking: what is anxiety telling us that might be useful? Do we need to give ourselves more time for a journey we're worried about, for instance? Sometimes, though, we feel anxious about the fact that we experience anxiety at all. That is an extra layer of anxiety you don't need.

When we are mindful, we notice anxiety when it arises. But we don't get anxious about being anxious; we don't build mental dramas on top of what's already there. We notice – then we move on to what, if anything, we can do next.

• Practice

When you feel anxiety, check if it's pointing towards something you need to do (send that email, maybe) and do it. If you can do nothing about the issue, try letting yourself experience the physical sensation of anxiety without scary self-talk. Then give your attention to whatever else you need to do in your day.

8 *Every step a liberation*

. . . .

Every step we take in mindfulness can help to liberate us from dwelling on the past, the future, our worries and our fears.

Imagine walking along, lost in thought about some long-past stressful event or about a drama that's going on at work. Now imagine walking while paying attention to the everyday things around you. In the first case, you're creating stress for yourself; in the second, you are allowing your surroundings to help you to move through your day without adding unnecessary stress to the moment.

• Practice
Now and then, as you move from one place to another, see if you can identify five things to be aware of. In an office you might be aware of the sky outside the window or of the sound of someone tapping on a keyboard, for instance. On the street you will easily spot things to be aware of – people, shop windows, perhaps trees. Rest your mind in these experiences.

9 *Does it really matter? Really?*

· · · · · · ·

Much of what we worry about doesn't really matter. Accepting and reminding ourselves of this can bring instant relief from constant fretting.

We have a strange habit of worrying about things that might be inconvenient or annoying, but that don't really matter. Yet that worry gets us stressed and damages our quality of life. For instance, maybe it doesn't matter all that much if you choose the wrong restaurant, miss the train or have lots of unanswered emails in your inbox; is it worth worrying about? Probably not – and when we practise mindful acceptance we can spot unnecessary worry and drop it.

• Practice

The way to practise this is with small inconveniences. Resolve that for twenty minutes you will ask yourself of worries that arise, 'Does it really matter? Really?' Of course, sometimes it really will. But I predict that you'll be surprised at how often it doesn't. Try to do this every day, at the same time.

10 *The mind is a poor fortune teller*

• • • • • • •

The mind is a poor fortune teller. Its predictions are often wrong again and again. That's worth remembering.

Newspapers have star racing tipsters who will tell you what's going to win the big race of the day. They are often wrong too. But does that lessen the air of authority with which they make the next day's predictions? Not in the least. The mind's like that as well. It will tell you with great 'certainty' what is going to happen, and it's wrong as often as it's right – none of which stops it from making its unreliable pronouncements with the greatest seriousness and authority.

● *Practice*
Next time you spot yourself believing in some painful future event as if it's definitely going to happen that way, remind yourself of those tipsters. I try to remember each day something my mind told me that turned out to be wrong – I easily got an extension on a project, though my mind told me I hadn't a hope, for instance. This helps me to be less trusting of its predictions.

11 *No-drama break*

· · · · · · ·

Put a little time aside now and then to practise experiencing minor imperfections and annoyances without creating a drama in your mind. This exercise can help you to live with less stress in an always-imperfect world.

One of our most deep-rooted traits is to feel annoyed when things turn out to be imperfect in a world filled with random events. Those who insist on perfection doom themselves to a lifetime of frustration. Of course, things go wrong that need to be put right – but not everything matters equally. When the garment you ordered online turns out to be the wrong size, for example, that is inconvenient and annoying, but it's probably not worth raising your blood pressure over it.

• *Practice*
Send yourself an email with the words 'No drama' in the subject line. Next time you spot it in your inbox, resolve that for an hour or so, you will not get into a drama in your head about minor annoyances. These include minor peculiarities of other people that normally irritate you.

12 *Email or breathing?*

Do you check your email more often than you check your breathing?

Most of the emails we receive can be ignored, but every now and then we get a genuinely interesting one that needs our attention. That's what makes checking the inbox so compulsive. Like a laboratory rat rewarded with a pellet of food every now and then after pressing a lever, we get 'rewarded' often enough to keep us checking.

Your email can drag you into many different states of mind, often stressful; your breathing brings you back to yourself. If you don't want to live like a laboratory rat, remember your breathing is at least as important as your email and give it some attention.

• *Practice*
Today, every time you think of checking your email, pause for long enough to check your breathing with full awareness. After that moment of returning to yourself, go ahead and look at your inbox if you absolutely have to. You will do so with a little more detachment.

13 *What do you appreciate?*

· · · · · · ·

We usually put more into getting an object or experience than we do into appreciating it when we have it. Appreciation isn't just a 'nice' idea: it's a way of getting more out of your life.

To appreciate something you have to pause and take it in. That's why appreciation makes a good mindfulness practice. Yet we race by, ignoring the good things in our lives. Is this down to our obsession with phones and other gadgets? No, it's not just an outcome of living in our busy, distracted era: the Danish philosopher Søren Kierkegaard wrote that most people run after pleasure so quickly they rush past it – and he was born in 1813.

● *Practice*
Wander around the space in which you live or work. Try to become aware of anything in it that you can appreciate. Then give a few moments to appreciating it. Remember, the key is that to appreciate you have to pause and take in what you normally pass by.

14   *Keep coming back*

· · · · · · · ·

Minds wander. If you try to keep your attention on your breath for one minute, you will catch your mind taking a sneaky excursion into the past or future. Being in the moment can bring you into calm – but you never get to stay in the moment for long. The trick is to keep coming back.

Mind wandering is often described as the brain's default mode. Daydreaming can be a pleasure, but wandering too often brings us into places of resentment, regret and fear. We can counteract it by coming into awareness of the present moment again and again. We're never perfect at this – wandering is the default mode – but the effort brings us the benefits of mindful calm.

• Practice
The more you practise mindfulness, the quicker you will notice when your attention has wandered off. Here's a simple practice: connect with the sensations in your hands and feet. Try holding both in your awareness for a while. While you are doing this, you are in the present moment.

15 *What's your intention?*

Do you know what your intention is at this moment? If you don't, you're drifting or daydreaming. If you do, you're aware.

Asking the question 'What's my intention?' brings you into mindful awareness immediately. You may be surprised by how often you have no idea what your intention is: you're on auto-pilot. As I've mentioned before, daydreaming is a pleasure, but if we want to make our dreams a reality, we have to move to aware intentions more often. Awareness of your intentions helps you to direct your energy well. In potential conflicts, it can help you to better navigate them. For instance, in a family meeting in which the behaviour of one person usually results in a row, remembering your intention to avoid one can enable you to take a deep breath instead of responding to provocations.

* *Practice*

Could you make a habit of asking yourself what your intention is each morning before you get out of bed? Could you send yourself an email with 'What's my intention?' in the subject line? Or write that question in a notebook or on your phone, where you will see it during the morning. And before you go to sleep at night, ask yourself 'What is my intention for tomorrow?'

16 *A small step back*

· · · · · · ·

Ever wished you had paused before you acted? Think of a pause
as taking a small step back. With mindfulness you train your
brain to pause more easily.

So much of our power as human beings lies in the pause.
Tennis players will often pause before making a crucial move,
for example. But as we go through day-to-day life, we often
forget to do this. The practice of mindfulness brings that 'not
rushing to judgement' to how we approach situations and
people. That is to say, we are less likely to be driven by old,
unhelpful reactions or assumptions. Spontaneity has its place
too, but the ability to take a small step back before acting never
loses its usefulness.

● *Practice*
Take a few moments now and then to bring your awareness to whatever is in your line of vision. When you see something that would
ordinarily get an immediate reaction from you, just hold off for a few
moments, breathe and observe. This 'something' might be no more
than an untidy bed or kitchen worktop. In this simple way, build your
capacity to take a small step back.

17 *From 'letting go' to 'letting be'*

One effective way to deal with an unpleasant thought is to 'let it be'. In other words, instead of thinking actively about it, give your attention to something fulfilling or useful. Then allow the thought to move on in its own time, in the background, so to speak.

In this case, you don't actively try to get rid of the thought or emotion. Instead you just avoid engaging or getting involved with it – you 'let it be', as you put your awareness on something useful or fulfilling.

• Practice

Imagine you are looking at the sky. Each thought that comes into your mind becomes a bird flying across it. Watch each bird flying across the sky until it becomes a dot in the distance and finally vanishes, bringing you back to a clear sky. You don't have to hurry the bird that carries your thought – let it cross in its own time. Meanwhile, notice the breath in your tummy and chest.

18 *A peaceful mind*

· · · · · · · ·

When your mind is churned up your thoughts swirl around like leaves in a storm. When your mind is peaceful it's like the surface of a lake in calm weather. Mindful awareness helps you to see which state your mind is in. It also helps you to notice when your mind is calm and to enjoy that for a while.

If your mind is at peace, hold off on introducing problems and issues for a little while if you can. Just let it be. Stop talking to yourself and focus for a while on your out-breath.

• *Practice*

Take a little time to visualise a lake, the water, the trees surrounding it, perhaps hills in the distance. If the lake reflected your mind, would it be choppy or at peace right now? If it's choppy, try turning your attention to your breath for a while and allow it to become calm. If it is already calm, try observing your out-breath or a physical sensation within that sense of calm and come back to it when you need to. The imaginary lake – or a lake you have been to and that you remember – can become a resource for you whenever you need it.

LABYRINTH → 3

19 *The good sailor*

A good sailor manages the boat but cannot command the sea. The outcome of a voyage depends both on the sea and on the sailor's choices. Life's like that too – so be compassionate to yourself.

Are choices pointless? No, sometimes the choices you make change everything. But sometimes they change very little. A lot depends on the strength of the circumstances you find yourself in. And since you are not all-knowing, you are unlikely to make the best possible choice every time. Moreover, you are not a robot: you are a human being with emotions, and they will also colour your choices. So, yes, be self-compassionate.

● *Practice*
Ask, 'What might be a better choice than what I'm doing now?' For example, if you've got an exam coming up, choosing to study for a while might be a better choice than sitting there criticising yourself for not studying. But note that word 'might'. You cannot know for sure – though I reckon it's pretty clear-cut in this case!

20 *Harsh critic to true friend*

• • • • • • •

Do you criticise yourself harshly for the simplest mistakes?
Many of us do, though not out loud. Instead, the criticism –
even condemnation – goes on inside our heads.

Harsh condemnation is of little help to you in living your life or
making necessary changes. Better the sort of friendly support
that I hope you would give to another person. The harsh critic
will often focus on events that you cannot change any more. A
friendly voice would be more likely to concentrate on changes
that are in your power to make. Try talking to yourself in a
friendly way. See the difference when you do.

• *Practice*
When you spot yourself being harshly critical of yourself, ask: 'Who's
talking now? Would I talk to a friend in this way? What would a true
friend say?' The answer can come quickly, and is usually more useful
than harsh criticism.

21 *Out of your head, into your body*

· · · · · · ·

Practising awareness of the present moment is so simple an activity it makes no sense that it should have such profound effects. But like a light touch on the tiller of a boat, it can change your whole direction.

To move often from what is happening in the world inside your head to what is going on outside your head or in your body can bring a sense of calm and spaciousness. This shift into the moment makes you present for your life and helps you to make better choices in the day. Is that all? No. It can also prevent you from turning small problems into huge dramas, so that they stay easy to deal with.

● *Practice*
Coming into the moment is easy. For instance, notice what your body is doing right now – is it standing, walking, running, lying down? Shifting awareness to your body in this way is one of the oldest of all mindfulness techniques, going back at least 2,000 years.

22 *Staying in touch*

· · · · · · ·

Sometimes finding peace in your day isn't a matter of going to a beautiful beach at sunrise. In our era of distraction, finding peace can mean pressing pause and coming into awareness of simple, unremarkable moments.

Staying in touch with life is a choice we need to make again and again. Why make that choice? Because otherwise we run the risk of living absurd lives in which we endlessly work for a tomorrow that never comes because we are never there for it: we are always on the way to someplace else. Every time you return to the moment – even an ordinary one – you get back in touch with your real life.

• *Practice*
Becoming aware of your breathing in the background can be a great way to maintain your present-moment awareness for longer periods before you become distracted. Think of keeping 10 per cent of your awareness on your breath. (Don't worry about whether it's actually 10 per cent or not – keep it simple!) Another – perhaps more pleasant – way to do this would be to take half an hour each day to do something that makes you feel peaceful; for instance, take a bath, read a book or make a cup of your favourite tea.

23 Old reruns

· · · · · · ·

When you find you're lost in a hurtful memory you've recalled many times before, step into awareness of the present moment and let the story fall away. Why? Because old stories can still hurt. They get the stress hormones flowing in your body, but they achieve nothing else.

We can get lost in these hurtful stories, memories or imaginings without warning. It's like waking up every so often in a cinema showing the same old movie. We don't always realise we can get up and leave. Sometimes we even stay for a few screenings. That's not worth the price of the ticket. Head for an exit and some fresh air.

● *Practice*

If you practise mindfulness, you will get good at realising you're lost in a story. Then, ask yourself if rerunning this story helps or hurts your quality of life? If it hurts, step into awareness of your present moment – of sounds, of what you see around you, of what you are physically doing. Remind yourself of how far you've come and how the experience made you the person you are today. Let the movie fade.

LABYRINTH → 14

24 *What's your mind telling you?*

•••••••

Ask yourself now and then: 'What's my mind telling me about this?' 'This' means whatever situation you are in or wherever you are right now.

The answer might surprise you. You don't have to analyse it, just notice. When you acknowledge what your mind is saying you might find it's grumbling to itself or repeating fearful thoughts. Sometimes you'll find that what your mind is saying has nothing to do with what's going on. Maybe it's in a bad mood. Or maybe it's reacting badly to something that happened years ago and isn't relevant anymore. Once you know, you are better placed to make choices based on today's reality.

• *Practice*
To remember this question, you need a little trigger, something that reminds you to ask it. For instance, you can practise asking the question when you're having your first coffee or tea of the day or when you're logging on to the computer system at work. Over time, asking yourself this question and tuning in to how you're feeling will become second nature.

25 *Important? Soon forgotten*

· · · · · · ·

Unless something really significant happened yesterday you probably haven't spent much time thinking about it today. Yet, at the time, passing events can seem terribly important. Of course, they matter in the sense that they form part of your life. However, remembering how quickly they will pass into forgetfulness can help you to take it all less seriously, lighten up, enjoy the good and laugh a little more.

● *Practice*
Look up a random date from the past year or so on the calendar on your phone and ask yourself: 'I wonder what I was worrying about on that date that seemed important, but that I can't remember now? How many of today's worries will I remember next year?' Then move on with your day with a lighter attitude, making sure to give attention to passing happy events also.

26 *To do or to be?*

Do you find you have to be doing something at all times? If you can't do anything – in a waiting room where you can't use your phone, say – do you fret? When, then, do you get to 'be'?

We are designed to want to do things. These include 'doing' activities like organising a work meeting and 'being' activities that satisfy us in themselves, like reading a novel. We need balance, but nowadays, this always seems to tip towards doing. Suppose you allowed yourself to 'be' from time to time? You would find oases of calm you don't even notice right now. To create a better balance we need to make deliberate choices again and again to 'be' without always having to achieve.

• *Practice*
For a few moments, think of yourself as 'being' rather than 'doing'. Enjoy the sensation of just listening to the sounds around you or experiencing the feeling of being alive. Commuting can provide an opportunity for this.

27 *Suspend judgement*

· · · · · · ·

Can you suspend judgement every so often and observe the reality of whatever it is that you're judging? You may find that holding off before rushing to judgement helps you to approach situations in new ways.

We make quick judgements all the time. This can be useful as we navigate our way through our days. But a day spent judging everything can also be a stressful day – when we react out of old habits and not on the basis of the reality of what is happening now. Not rushing to judgement is a key part of mindfulness practice. This allows us a moment to observe situations, and our own reactions, before we act.

● *Practice*
What can you see in your surroundings right now that you would ordinarily judge very quickly, whether favourably or unfavourably? This could be a person, a photograph, perhaps a document relating to your work. Can you observe silently in your mind for a short while without repeating your usual judgements? Is there another point of view you could have?

28 Check in with your hunger

Do you find you eat too much of the food you describe in your darker moments as 'rubbish'? Learning to check in with your stomach to find out if it's actually hungry could make all the difference. This is a way to bring mindfulness to the practical aspects of your life.

We often eat for emotional reasons – comfort food, for instance – even when we are not hungry. We all know this, but we easily forget to check with the stomach to see if it really wants to be fed. Very often, it's the emotions that are hungry, but the stomach is not.

• Practice
When you're feeling 'peckish', check if your stomach is hungry or if it's all in the mind. When you're eating, eat with awareness, so you know when you're full; and after you enjoy a pleasant meal, bring your awareness to the satisfied feeling in your stomach.

29   *Switch to neutral*

· · · · · · ·

Accepting unpleasant realities that are out of your control is a
basic skill of mindfulness, and one that can lighten your path as
you go through your day.

Sometimes it's as if there is a switch in our brains that makes us
struggle against everything when it's on and accept everything
when it's off (I've borrowed this idea from Acceptance and
Commitment Therapy – ACT). The neutral setting is probably
best. This means pausing to figure out what's worth pouring
energy into and what's not: if your car breaks down when you're
on the school run, you need to struggle – get a lift or ask
another parent to help; but if you're delayed by a broken traffic
light on the way home from work, a struggle is pointless.

• *Practice*
Looking ahead at today, can you anticipate anything you're tempted
to struggle with but that doesn't matter all that much? It's easier to
practise on situations that aren't important – and you may even be
surprised at how many of the situations you struggle with in your
mind, or even out loud, aren't really important after all. If you can
learn to accept discomfort, you'll live a calmer, happier life. Save your
energies for what really matters.

30 *Under pressure*

∙∙∙∙∙∙∙

When you feel under pressure, bring awareness without words
to your body. By 'without words', I mean stop talking to yourself
for a few moments and just connect with yourself as a physical
being.

When we feel hurried and harried we almost forget that we
have bodies. We get so caught up in what's going on in our
heads that we 'become' that pressure. Awareness of the body
immediately gives us a sense of perspective, a little space, and
allows us to physically relax, even as we deal with the situation.
Body awareness means letting go of the mind's chatter by
moving your awareness to your head, your trunk, your arms and
your legs.

∙ *Practice*
You can bring awareness to your body by feeling the chair underneath
you, listening to the sounds around you and being conscious of the
ground beneath your feet. You are more likely to be able to do this if
you frequently practise coming into body awareness during the day.

31 *Break those chains*

· · · · · · · ·

Unhelpful chains of thought can bring our moods down before we've noticed what's going on. Cultivating the practice of returning awareness to your breathing or your body, even for moments at a time, helps to break these often harmful chains.

When it comes to the mind, one thing leads to another. Your twelve-year-old is grumpy and you wonder if you've failed as a parent, if she's always going to hate you and so on and on. Keep it going and you could end up snapping at your aggrieved twelve-year-old for no obvious reason. The same applies to thinking about mistakes you made in the past, connecting one to another like a toxic daisy chain, convincing yourself, ridiculously, that you're a monster.

• *Practice*
By doing mindfulness practices, we get really good at spotting what's going on and then we can choose to break the chain. One way to do this is to bring your focus to your fingers, one at a time, and breathe in and out twice for each finger of each hand.

32 *What you haven't got*

· · · · · · ·

Focusing on what you haven't got is sometimes necessary. Out of teabags? You might need to focus on getting more – certainly in my house! But too much focus on what you haven't got harms your emotional wellbeing. So try to bring appreciation of what you have into the day also.

A life without appreciation seems rather limited and bleak. We don't need to go around singing a happy song in all possible circumstances. But by replacing some of our complaints about what we haven't got with appreciation of what we have, we enhance our overall experience of life.

• *Practice*
Cultivate daily appreciation as a mindfulness practice. When you go for a walk or when you're on a plane, bus or train, take a few minutes for mindfulness. Observe your breathing, and ask yourself, 'What do I appreciate?' It might be what you appreciate in the present moment or what you appreciate in your life. Make a short list – just a few things will do. You could make this list part of a gratitude diary if you keep one.

33 *Never a dull moment?*

People who practise mindfulness are quite fond of dull moments. Why? Because returning to a dull moment (of which, you'll be glad to hear, you'll never run short) strengthens your mindfulness capacity. It's like running up a slope to strengthen your legs.

People can't bear dull moments – just look around you: usually they dive into their phones because they cannot tolerate a minute that isn't filled with interesting events. But being able to return to and tolerate dull moments rewards us with greater calm and clarity in our lives. They're not much fun though, are they, dull moments? And this is not an appeal for you to spend all your time in them. However, try to mindfully accept dullness even for a minute or so when it descends.

● *Practice*
Next time you find yourself in a dull moment, whether you're in a waiting room, sitting at home or in the workplace, pause before you rush on. Let yourself physically relax into the experience. Allow your-self a nice, long out-breath. Then escape if you still need to.

34 *Catastrophe? Outrageous? Not really*

· · · · · · ·

One way to increase your stress is to describe the normal inconveniences and disappointments of life as 'catastrophic', 'outrageous', 'devastating' or 'completely unacceptable'. Very few events in your daily life can accurately be described in these terms. For instance, if the train is half an hour late because of leaves on the line, that's inconvenient and annoying, but not catastrophic.

Emotional language is often exaggerated – especially when we talk to ourselves. The inconvenient becomes catastrophic, the annoying outrageous, the disappointing devastating and someone else stepping out of line becomes completely unacceptable (even though you are going to accept it). Does that really matter, though? Yes: because telling your brain that something is catastrophic is a good way to make it fearful – and when it gets fearful, the stress hormones start to flow.

• *Practice*
Watch your language. When you find yourself using dramatic, exaggerated emotional words – as we all do in our heads – take a moment to question what you're saying and, if appropriate, to change it.

35 *What's likely to happen?*

. . . .

When we are very anxious about something it can help to ask and answer a few structured questions. These are about what you fear will happen, what you hope will happen and what is likely to happen.

Asking structured questions is a good way to work with anxiety – they channel your thoughts in a useful direction instead of allowing them to flow into catastrophic scenarios. In the exercise below, when you ask yourself 'What do I fear will happen?' I advise you not to dwell on the answer for too long: we are trying to avoid getting lost in rumination, not to encourage it!

● *Practice*
Ask yourself these three questions:

• What do I fear will happen? (Don't dwell on this.)
• What do I hope will happen? (It's fine to dwell on this.)
• What do I expect will actually happen? (The answer to this most likely falls somewhere between the two previous answers. It can bring you back to a sense of proportion and balance.)

36 *From mind to body*

....

In our lives, we feel many unwelcome emotions: anger, sadness
or fear, for instance. Very often, you will find it helpful to experience the emotion in your body instead of thinking about it.
The mind exaggerates emotions, but when you turn your attention to what they feel like in your body, they will usually
become easier to bear.*

Body awareness promotes calm and keeps you in the present
moment with the benefits this can bring. Calm breathing –
especially a nice, long out-breath – adds to the stress-reduction
effect.

• Practice
When you find yourself lost in thought or emotion, come into an
awareness of your body. One way to do this is to notice how your
chest and tummy expand and settle back as you breathe in and out.
This exercise also helps you to notice if you are physically tense and
to relax: often, awareness alone is enough to bring about relaxation.

* If you suffer from post-traumatic stress, and if going into the
physical sensation makes you feel uneasy, then use the other ideas
in the book instead.

37 *Worry vs acceptance*

• • • • • • •

If you're worrying about today, ask yourself what you should really worry about and what you should accept. You might be surprised at the difference this makes.

When you do this simple exercise you will probably find a tendency to worry not only about what's important but also about problems that don't matter. For the latter, try acceptance as your first option. Not sure you'll easily find parking when you drive to a meeting? Accept it and leave early or take the train. For problems that matter, it helps to distinguish between what's in your control, e.g. the parking problem, and what's outside it: was your promotion interview successful? It's now outside your control. Remind yourself of this instead of worrying about it.

• *Practice*
When I take a walk I like to ask myself two questions: what am I aware of? What do I accept? The first is a mindfulness awareness exercise: what do I see, hear, feel – such as a breeze, clouds, etc.? The second is usually about today's events. Maybe I've got to do something that bores me or that I find dissatisfying or scary. But if I accept that this is so, I can stop arguing with reality and either do it or drop it.

LABYRINTH → 10

38 *Well-wishing*

· · · · · · · ·

We have a 'me, me, me' tendency in which we relate everything to ourselves. It probably evolved as a survival mechanism. But self-preoccupation can also lead us deep into emotional places that are bad for us, pushing us towards feeling depressed, for instance.

One function of the brain is to relate the external world to ourselves. This is necessary to our wellbeing: that red traffic light isn't just a dramatic colour – it's a signal to me to stop! But when it goes too far we become cut off from awareness of other people and our moods can go down. Directing attention to other people with a wishing-well exercise will help you to step out of the stream of self-preoccupation. Try the traditional practice below.

● *Practice*
Think of somebody you like or love. Visualise them sitting in front of you. Now silently wish them well: 'Be happy, be safe, be well.' Now think of somebody towards whom you have no strong feelings. Again, wish them well: 'Be happy, be safe, be well.' Finally, wish yourself well: 'Be happy, be safe, be well.' Do this practice at least once a week to allow it to become a habit – it's worth it.

39 *Let me be imprecise*

· · · · · · ·

The philosophy behind mindfulness accepts that everything is changing all the time and that reality cannot conform precisely to what you want. Today, when considering if events, items and people meet your expectations, leave a margin for acceptable error.

Buddhist philosophy – from which mindfulness in the West is adapted – holds that everything is impermanent. This includes not only objects, but also emotions, thoughts and intentions. In such a world, to demand perfection of ourselves or others is unrealistic. Of course, we can work to improve our experiences and those of the people we love, but if we demand precision in human affairs, we will generate unhappiness.

● *Practice*
Do you have something that is a little broken or worn – not 'perfect', so to speak – but that you like anyway? Could you put it somewhere you can see it every day? And decide that every time you see it, this object will remind you that perfection and precision are not required for satisfaction?

40 Morita: driven by purpose

. . . .

Feelings and purposes are often not in harmony. A key to moving forward is to allow your purpose to guide you while fully acknowledging your feelings.

A century ago, Japanese psychiatrist Dr Shoma Morita encouraged people held back by shyness and nervousness to base their actions on purpose rather than feeling. His approach included the formula 'Know your purpose, acknowledge your feelings, do what needs to be done.' If your purpose is to go to the party and your feeling is shyness, what needs to be done is that you go to the party as a shy person. Feelings can drive out awareness of purpose. Morita's formula puts your purpose behind the steering wheel, while accepting that your feelings will be along for the ride.

● *Practice*
When lack of confidence or shyness gets in the way, ask: 'What's my purpose; what are my feelings; what needs to be done?' Then, if the purpose is valid, do what needs to be done, while acknowledging your feelings.

41 *Draw the line*

· · · · · · ·

If you imagine you are drawing a familiar object – a cup, ornament, book, vase – you may notice details you have never been aware of before.

People who take up drawing quickly discover that we usually only 'see' a simplified version of reality. When we look at objects, people or animals we omit lines, angles, shadows, even some colours. A good mindfulness exercise to illustrate this and bring you more fully into present-moment experience is to imagine you are drawing something and look for the lines, colours and shadows you would include. You will experience an immediate, deeper awareness of everyday objects and an interesting new mindfulness practice.

● *Practice*
Observe any familiar object in your line of vision. Draw it with your eyes. Consider what details you should outline. What dark and bright areas would you include? Maintain a background awareness of your breathing as you are doing this.

42 *A weighty matter*

• • • • • • •

Noticing the weight of everyday objects is an exercise in pure awareness. Try it with cups of tea or coffee today, or with your phone if you carry it in your hand.

Mindfulness doesn't have to be complicated. It's about bringing your attention back to awareness of your experience in this moment, and doing so again and again, because awareness always drifts. People who practise mindfulness daily do so by becoming aware of something they sense – breath, sounds, posture, for instance. Many never think of awareness of weight as an aid to mindfulness. Yet to be aware of weight you must focus on it in this moment. We lift or carry all sorts of objects all the time – a simple, no-fuss awareness of their weight will turn this everyday action into a mindfulness practice.

• *Practice*
Pick up three objects that are near you right now. Notice their differing weights. Get into the habit of noticing the weights of books, cups and other everyday objects. This straightforward and slightly odd exercise brings you straight into mindfulness of the everyday – which is where you live your life.

43 *Just say no?*

·······

Lots of us are scared of saying 'no'. If you're unhappy about something you need to do in the days ahead, could it be something you should have said 'no' to? And if you should've said 'no' then, could you still say it now?

If you don't say 'no' often enough, why is that? Maybe you see yourself as a 'can-do', always helpful person. Or maybe you fear upsetting other people? If you're saying 'yes' too often, you need to do something about this. Bear in mind that sometimes people just want to be heard and respected and if you say 'no' in a respectful way, they will very often be fine with that. And sometimes – to your surprise – you'll find that people are just not all that bothered when you say 'no'.

• Practice
The more you cultivate mindfulness, the more likely you are to pause before saying 'yes' or 'no'. Practise remaining mindful in day-to-day conversations, especially with people who demand a lot from you.

44 *Eat your way to mindfulness*

· · · · · · · ·

Mindful eating means knowing that you're eating while you're eating. In other words, bringing awareness to the taste of your food. It takes you into the reality of the moment in a pleasant way, several times a day.

For most of us, eating is not just about removing hunger. It is also an emotional act: if you're anxious, you might eat lots of comfort food, for instance. So bringing mindful awareness to your eating can heal emotions, as well as enhancing the experience of eating. No need to eat terribly slowly – it's about paying attention to the experience.

● *Practice*
Do you sometimes eat alone? If so, try to bring awareness to the experience, the taste, the texture and the aroma. Choose your food with care. When eating with others bring awareness to your food when you put it in your mouth. If snacking, give some attention to your food also – walking around eating a snack with your mind somewhere else is pointless.

45 *Your mindful space*

· · · · · · · ·

You can have your own mindfulness space, only it's probably
not going to be a private temple. Decide to be mindful in a
certain part of your home – bedroom, kitchen, bathroom, living
room, garden – and that part of your home will come to be
your mindfulness space.

As we go through a familiar place, such as our home, it's easy to
become preoccupied and almost to go around in a trance. But if
one room in your home is designated by you as a space for
mindful awareness, then simply crossing the threshold will
bring you back to awareness. And you don't have to live in a
grand home with a beautiful garden and a musical fountain for
this to work. All you need is a space – it could even be the
shower!

● *Practice*
Choose a space in your home – though outside is fine too – and
whenever you are in that space, come into awareness of where you
are and what you are doing. Value that moment.

46 *Welcoming happiness*

· · · · · · ·

If you are happy right now or if you experience happy moments later today or tomorrow, be alert to the presence of happiness and give it a warm welcome.

We may create conditions in our lives that we hope will lead to happiness, but it's not guaranteed to arrive on schedule and we cannot dictate how long it will stay. So it is ridiculous to be upset because you are not happy in this particular moment. What's even more ridiculous is to notice you are happy and then ignore it. If happiness comes as a gift to you, awareness is the gift you give to happiness.

● *Practice*

Think of something in your life that makes you feel positive, even if it's just a tiny light in the darkness. When you think of it how do you feel? And what does your breathing feel like? By coming into the appreciation of positivity in this way, you are more likely to recognise happiness when it visits.

47 *Be kind to your future self*

· · · · · · ·

What can you do now that your future self will be grateful for?
Maybe you need to make a phone call you've been putting off,
or tidy up your room or start work you've been avoiding. Think
of these actions as kindnesses to your future self.

Self-compassion involves kindness towards yourself – not as a
reward for doing well, but for its own sake. One way to be a
friend to yourself is to do future kindnesses. If you've got to be
at the airport at 6 a.m., it will be kinder to go to bed early than
to go out on the town, for instance.

• Practice

Can you build an action into your routine to be kind to yourself? For
example, can you set up breakfast the night before, so you can eat
before going to work? Can you walk at lunchtime, so that the 'you' of
the afternoon will have more energy? Think small actions – they make
a big difference.

48 *Practising unhappiness*

....

Practising to be unhappy sounds daft, doesn't it? But when you sit there going over the things that annoy you, things you cannot or will not do anything about, isn't that exactly what you are doing? What would it feel like to think about positive aspects of your day or your life instead?

Practice makes perfect and that's the trouble. Keeping up that monologue of grumbling and complaining can make you an expert in the art of bringing your mood down to your boots and keeping it there. It can also get you caught in a loop of rumination (repeating angry, sad or fearful thoughts over and over) and that can push you into a worse mood, whether towards depression (which it can worsen if you're already depressed) or anger.

● *Practice*
Next time you catch yourself mulling over some annoyance that you've gone over more often than is useful, tell your mind to 'stop wasting my time', then switch your attention and redirect it to something – anything – in your environment.

49 *Beyond control*

· · · · · · ·

Feelings are not in your direct control. Putting your focus on what you actually do (mindful walking or drinking a cup of tea in awareness) is a behaviour you can carry out regardless of how you feel.

Sometimes our feelings tell us helpful things ('I love this person and I want to do something nice for them') and sometimes not ('Don't go into the dentist's surgery – run away now!'). Accepting the presence of our feelings can bring a degree of calm, and this makes it easier to work out how to respond to them – or whether we need to respond at all.

• *Practice*
Imagine you have emotional traffic lights: green means feeling positive; red is for an unwanted feeling – stress, for instance; amber means you are moving from one state to another. Check in now and then with where you are. If you're in orange, note which direction you're going in. If you are heading for red, accept your feeling and rest your mind in your breath for a few moments. If you're heading towards green, be glad!

50 *The anchor*

· · · · · · · ·

Awareness of your breath is an excellent practice except that it's a rather general concept. Being specific through awareness of the breath in your nose, your throat, chest or tummy is more effective because it's easier to focus on a point.

Mindful awareness is helped by being specific: a sound, for example (birdsong, music, children playing) or an object (a parking meter near his office is the mindfulness object for one person I know). I think of these as 'anchors': they can pull you back into awareness. For mindfulness of the breath, it's really helpful to be specific and the more you use a specific point – nose, throat, chest or tummy – the more effective the practice will become.

● *Practice*
Pause for a few moments now and notice your breath at the anchor point. Don't do anything special with it. Just notice. Try it next when you are in a queue, waiting for a traffic light to change or if you've woken up during the night.

LABYRINTH → 30

51 *My happiness does not depend on this*

· · · · · · ·

What's on your mind at the moment? Does your happiness depend on it? What were you thinking about this day last year that you thought your happiness depended on? Do you even remember what it was?

Of course we don't go around saying, 'My happiness depends on getting what I want right now.' Yet we can so easily tense up and stress out as if our happiness was so fragile it depended on the most unimportant things: my new phone being delivered today, being able to book a table at that restaurant, meeting this deadline, catching that plane, selling this project and so on and on. Watch out for this tendency to treat these events as something they are not – namely as dictating our life's happiness

● *Practice*
When you're worrying about something or feeling uptight about it, remind yourself that, in all probability, 'My happiness does not depend on this.' Notice how this statement immediately lowers your stress level.

52 *Label negative feelings as unwanted*

· · · · · · · ·

If you have what you would normally call a 'negative' feeling, think of it instead as 'unwanted'.

Feelings such as anxiety, anger and sadness are usually labelled as 'negative'. However, in reality, they are only negative if they are harmful. Dwelling on anger regarding a past event you can do nothing about is negative, but anger about an unfair situation you can do something useful and appropriate about can be a positive force. This isn't splitting hairs; seeing a 'negative' feeling as 'unwanted and useful' or 'unwanted and unhelpful' can make it far easier to handle.

• *Practice*
When you spot a so-called 'negative' feeling – and they usually make their presence felt – remind yourself that it's actually an 'unwanted' feeling that may be helpful or unhelpful. See the difference this makes to how you relate to it and to how you deal with situations in which these feelings arise.

53 *Put a name on it*

• • • • • • •

Labelling fear, anger and other painful emotions reduces their intensity. If you're feeling a painful emotion, try putting a name on it: 'anxious', 'annoyed', 'sad', for instance. Just name it without dwelling on it, without wallowing in it.

It isn't clear why labelling emotions is helpful to us. It may be that it moves some of our energy and attention from the emotional part of the brain to the 'thinking' part. It's also helpful to name the emotion with the intention of turning down the volume, so to speak, of reducing the intensity. We can't control emotions, so don't expect this exercise to make them go away. But turning down the volume can bring welcome relief.

• *Practice*
What are you feeling right now? What's a one-word label for it? Calm? Apprehensive? Cheerful? Disappointed? Silently say the name of the emotion. Remember, you want to label your emotions, not analyse them or get lost in a series of reactions to them.

54 *Wait your way to calm*

· · · · · · ·

At any given time, you're probably waiting for something –
a delivery, an answer to a request, maybe. You'll never stop
waiting while you're alive. But instead of letting waiting be
a source of stress can you make it a source of calm?

We are born to wait. From the baby waiting for food to the
tycoon waiting for the conclusion of a mega-deal, we're having
waiting experiences. The more impatient you are, the more
stress you build up in your body. You can do yourself a favour
by practising calm awareness when you're waiting. This will
reduce the stress points in the day.

● *Practice*
What makes you feel impatient? Waiting for the computer system to
load at work? Sitting at a red traffic light? Turn it into an opportunity
for relaxed awareness: do some mindful breathing or walk to the
window while the computer system is cranking up; count how long
the traffic light stays red for (you might be surprised).

LABYRINTH → 26

55 *What's done is done*

It's a symptom of our over-committed age that so few of us can get to the end of the day or the week with a sense of satisfaction at a job well done. What did you complete yesterday or today, big or small? Can you give yourself some appreciation for that?

With every extra day you live, you've done more in your life. Isn't it a pity, then, to focus mainly on what you haven't done? Whether you've washed the dishes or created a new algorithm, you've done something. Couldn't you allow yourself to take a little pleasure in it? A good boss acknowledges the work of his or her staff. A good parent acknowledges the efforts of his or her child. Do it for yourself too.

● *Practice*
Run through a mental list of things you've done today. If you like written lists, jot them down. Now shift your focus from what you haven't done to what you've done. Allow yourself to acknowledge what you've accomplished.

56 *Change the destination*

Stressful thoughts can quickly lead you down a path of gloom or anger, increasing your blood pressure and lowering your well-being. So be aware of where your thoughts are going. If they habitually bring you into stressful places, try changing them.

For instance: 'Padraig will be at the meeting today' could lead to, 'He said that thing behind my back last year. That's the afternoon ruined for me.' If you spot this, you can change the second thought: 'Padraig will be at the meeting today. I'm not going to ruin my day by dwelling on him.'

• *Practice*
Notice what you're thinking right now. Now ask yourself, 'What's the next thought?' Could it be a different one? For instance: 'I've got to leave early today to collect my child. My colleagues will think I'm shirking.' Now substitute a new thought: 'I've got to leave early today to collect my child. This is the right choice for me and my child right now.'

57 *What's happening now?*

When you're being mindful you're being aware of what's happening now, in this moment. So what's happening now? I can hear a strong wind blowing outside and music playing in the next room. What's happening where you are? That's your moment.

You don't need to climb a mountain to practise mindfulness. You practise by bringing awareness to the ordinary details of your daily life. That can be at home, in the workplace or wherever else your day brings you. It's nice, of course, to go to mountains, beaches and retreats and practise some mindfulness there. But you're going to have to come home at some point (unless you live on a mountain, a beach or in a retreat centre) and it's the details of that ordinary life in your familiar places that really count.

• *Practice*
Notice your breathing. Now notice the feeling of your feet against the soles of your shoes, notice what you hear, what you see. What else are your senses bringing you?

LABYRINTH → 13

58 *The body scan*

· · · · · · ·

Awareness of your body without judgement can lower stress and calm emotions immediately. That's why the body scan has already been used by thousands of people around the world today.

If you pay attention to your emotions, you will notice that each one has a physical aspect. Anxiety might tense up your stomach, when you're calm your muscles might be more relaxed and so on. What this means is that calming your body can contribute to calming your emotions. So building the body scan into your day even for a few minutes can have profound effects.

• Practice
Bring your awareness to your toes. Now move up along your body with your awareness: feet, legs, back, chest, stomach, arms, hands, shoulders, head and then face. Allow yourself to relax as you do this – the relaxation will come naturally, just allow it. Imagine your whole body is breathing calmly now. Rest in awareness of your breathing body for at least a few moments, but for longer if you want.

59 *Pleasant, unpleasant, neutral*

• • • • • • •

Here's an easy way to look at the events of the day, taken from Buddhist psychology: some of its events will be pleasant, some will be unpleasant and some will be neutral. Can you enjoy the pleasant, accept the unpleasant and bring the neutral events into awareness more often?

Breaking the day down like this can save emotional energy, especially in accepting unpleasant events you've got to go through anyway. And your day will be richer if this approach reminds you to give attention and awareness to what is pleasant instead of passing it by. But remember to notice the neutral events too, those which don't generate any strong feelings in you, as these can provide great practice in coming into mindfulness.

• *Practice*
Try noticing neutral aspects of your experience: the houses you pass, everyday sounds from another room, people who serve you in the shop. Often it's these events we pay least attention to. Instead we wander off into rumination and into unhelpful memories and fears.

60 *What's your cue?*

. . . .

To come into mindfulness is easy but, as I've mentioned else-where, it is also very easy to forget to do it. One of the easiest ways to remember is to choose a few routine activities (maybe brushing your teeth) and deciding that you will always perform that activity mindfully.

Here's a list of possibilities: drinking tea or coffee, commuting, starting the car, washing your hands, showering, eating, walking the dog, walking to your workstation, waiting for your computer system to fire up, entering passwords, playing with your child, locking your door, using the stairs, resting your head on the pillow at night.

● *Practice*
Start early in the day. For instance, bring mindful awareness to commuting or walking to work. Instead of thinking about this morn-ing's meeting, bring your awareness to driving, cycling, the view from a train and so on for at least part of the time. If you don't go out to work, then opening your curtains or making coffee could be your cue.

61 *What do you see?*

· · · · · · · ·

Use visualisation to become more calm and grounded. For example, imagine you are observing a garden that reflects your emotions. If you're feeling agitated, perhaps the flowers are being bent over by the wind and you can sit and wait for the wind and your emotions to settle.

How do you see the day ahead in your mind's eye? How do you see yourself in that day? Perhaps you see yourself being run ragged in a busy day – an unpleasant feeling to start off with. Perhaps you could replace it with an image of you working diligently and peacefully. This brings a little calm and distance and you might even see solutions such as getting more help, extending deadlines or dropping some tasks. Even observing a quick mental image now and then of yourself relaxing into mindful breathing will make a difference.

• *Practice*
Imagine a garden that's driven by your current emotions. What's happening? Is it caught in a storm or is it placid? If a storm is blowing, perhaps you can wait for it to become calm? If it's peaceful, enjoy the colours and scents of the flowers.

62 Touch mindfulness

· · · · · · ·

Touch might be the fastest route into mindfulness because it is always in the here and now. Notice where one surface touches another – your back against the chair, your feet against the soles of your shoes, for instance.

The touch of a loved one is calming. A parent hugging a distressed child uses the power of touch. If you're lying awake in bed at night, awareness of the touch of the bedclothes against your body can take your mind off your worries and get you back to sleep. Becoming aware of the often-ignored world of touch can deepen your experience of living – and it can do so straight away.

· *Practice*
Deliberately practise awareness of touch, maybe noticing the feel of your clothes, your partner's hand, your feet against the soles of your shoes, even the touch of the air in your nostrils. What's your body touching now? Why not take yourself on a walk during which you will cultivate an awareness of touch?

63 *Step off the hedonic treadmill*

· · · · · · ·

We have an odd habit of giving too little awareness to the pleasures of life. What's pleasurable in your day today that you could bring mindful awareness to experiencing?

Taking pleasures for granted and then seeking new ones is described as the 'hedonic treadmill'. 'Hedonic' refers to pleasure and happiness. It's a human characteristic to take pleasures for granted when we've got them and to go looking for new ones – which we will take for granted in their turn. That's the treadmill. How to get off? One answer is to deliberately pause to enjoy what we've got – books languishing in the shadows for years, beautiful dishware we hardly notice, music we say we love but haven't listened to in ages.

● *Practice*
Look for objects or experiences (music, for instance) that used to give you pleasure but that you barely notice anymore. Can you pause and 'enjoy' the pleasure, bringing these familiar objects and experiences back to life for you again, so to speak?

64 *What's your poison?*

· · · · · · ·

What 'musts' do you have in your day? In other words, what routines and activities do you think you 'must' have? These 'musts' are attachments that can limit your experience of life.

'Set in their ways' is a phrase sometimes applied to someone who won't tolerate change. A young person who 'must' get smashed on alcohol every Friday night is also 'set in their ways'. Attachments lead us through life without having to try new things or make new choices. In that way they deprive us of a whole world of experience.

● *Practice*
Spot less helpful attachments. Do you have a route to work that you 'must' take? Do you have a certain order in which you 'must' do things? Are there interesting experiences you deny yourself (or your partner) because you are so attached to your routine?

65 *The power of asking*

· · · · · · ·

If you are really under pressure, you won't want to do this, but you should: ask somebody for something. That 'something' could be practical help, a listening ear or advice.

One way to get burned out, where you cannot function healthily anymore, is to take on more and more, until you run yourself into the ground. Our expectations of ourselves can be unrealistically demanding, and it is easier than you might think to get into the spiral leading to emotional exhaustion, especially in a poorly managed environment. Asking is the first step towards breaking the spiral. The most powerful people in the world ask for what they want. It is strength, not weakness.

● *Practice*
Try asking yourself:

● What would it be ok to ask for? Let's suppose the answer is a three-day extension on the submission date for your project.
● What else? Postponing a new project for a couple of weeks.
● When will I ask? The sooner the better – before you scare yourself out of asking!

66 *Deliberate stillness*

· · · · · · ·

When was the last time you had a deliberate moment of stillness? Don't be pushed and pulled through your day today. Look
for moments of stillness that help you to come home to yourself.

Lovers are still when they're gazing into each other's eyes. Tens
of thousands of people are still when they're waiting for a
crucial penalty to be taken. But these are special moments. For
too much of the time we're like spinning tops set whirling by
the demands and distractions of the day. But when do you get
to enjoy the presence of someone you love or to figure out if
what you're getting is what you want?

• Practice
Deliberate stillness is an act of autonomy on your part. To come
quickly into stillness, rest your awareness on your out-breath, allowing
stillness in with it. The out-breath engages the part of your nervous
system (the parasympathetic nervous system) that calms you down. It
is very helpful in inducing moments of stillness.

67 *A stone in your shoe*

· · · · · · ·

If you're suffering emotional pain, and if that pain is going to be with you for some time, you still need to get things done. Try looking on the pain as a stone in your shoe: you hurt, but you can still move on with what you need to do.

The concept of emotional pain as a stone in your shoe helps you to see that such pain need not always immobilise you. Sometimes you need to cry, to lick your wounds. But sometimes also you can allow the pain to accompany you while you do whatever has to be done in the day or just for the next five minutes. In doing so, you can acknowledge and respect the pain.

● *Practice*

If you carry emotional pain, be careful not to get lost in it for longer than is needed (how long that is will vary from person to person). Acknowledge it as 'a stone in my shoe' and continue on your journey through your day.

68 *Three drivers*

• • • • • • •

Think of yourself as having three motivational systems: 'goal-seeking', 'fight or flight' and 'tend and befriend'. Give your 'tend-and-befriend' system some attention today in relation to yourself – it's the one that easily gets forgotten.

Our strongest drive as human beings is the one we share with other creatures: survival. That's why we can go into 'fight-or-flight' mode instantly when we perceive a threat. 'Goal-seeking' is what we direct much of our energy towards at other times. 'Tend and be-friend' is caregiving or, when applied to ourselves, self-compassion. It's easy for the other two systems to push self-compassion aside. Sometimes that's necessary – survival comes first and goal-seeking can require pushing ourselves hard. That's why we need to make self-compassion a deliberate pursuit, otherwise it can get lost.

• *Practice*
Before you sleep tonight ask yourself what you can do to befriend yourself tomorrow? Make it something easily doable. For instance, you could set aside twenty minutes to have a cup of tea or coffee and to read your favourite magazine; you could plan to take a pleasant walk at lunchtime; or you could take the time to plan an enjoyable dinner. When you get up in the morning, take a moment to remind yourself of what you've planned.

LABYRINTH → 40

69 *What are the odds?*

. . . .

The human population of the planet is about seven and a half thousand million. So far as we know, nobody's perfect. This means the odds against you being perfect are approximately seven and a half thousand million to one.

One of the mysteries of human life is a tendency to expect perfection from ourselves while, at the same time, knowing that human beings are just not perfect. If you remember this, it can help you to break the sense of isolation that comes from thinking you are unique in being flawed. Of course, we don't think that way logically – it's more like an unexamined thought in the back of the mind. It is also an unhelpful thought that can bring a great deal of unhappiness, and we really owe it to ourselves to challenge it.

● *Practice*
Try noting the everyday faults of people you know – not with annoyance, but with humour. Now think of some minor faults of your own and try to take the same attitude towards those.

70 *Light in the cellar*

· · · · · · ·

When you make a habit of dwelling on painful memories you repeat your suffering again and again. If you find yourself drawn to these memories, try to bring happy ones into the picture also.

In traditional Buddhist psychology we are thought to have a cellar (called Alaya) in our psyche, which contains seeds from our past experience. They live in the dark unless we shine a light on them. If we shine the light on painful memories, their seeds come to life in the form of suffering. So we need to be careful of what we dwell on from the past. But remember we can also choose to give time and energy to dwelling on happy memories.

● *Practice*
If you tend towards the painful in your memory, take the time to recollect a few happy memories. Make a list if it helps. Then, when you find yourself lost in a sad or anger-provoking memory, try to follow it with a happy one from your list.

71 Two arrows

. . . .

Think of a painful event, big or small, as an arrow that suddenly strikes you. When the wound heals or the pain dies down, do you continue to 'dwell' on that event, going over and over and over it in your mind? That's a second arrow that you stick into yourself. Can you accept instead that the painful event happened, do whatever you need to do that helps and then move on with your life?

This is not to deny that an injustice may need to be righted and a traumatic event, physical or emotional, may need treatment. What we are concerned with here are those other events, big or small, that hurt us and that we keep alive by dwelling on them perhaps for years and even decades, often only harming ourselves further in the process.

• Practice
How many 'first arrows' did yesterday send? Can you let at least some of them 'be'? In other words, acknowledge the painful event without talking endlessly to yourself about it?

72 Contrition is ok, and it helps

• • • • • • • •

If you hurt somebody and it's your fault, you could wallow in self-hatred, but that won't do any good. Or you could figure out spurious reasons why it wasn't your fault in the first place, and that won't do any good either. It's ok to feel contrition, to say you're sorry and, if you can, to make amends.

We rub each other up the wrong way and, in the process, we hurt and offend each other. That's how it is with humans. We have innumerable different expectations, perceptions and ways of doing things. So sometimes we do, indeed, need to feel contrite when we infringe on other people's rights or hurt them in some way.

• Practice
If there's something you ought to feel sorry for, then it's ok to feel sorry for it. Instead of trying to think up excuses, figure out what you will do the next time anything like this arises. And consider saying 'sorry' to the injured party.

LABYRINTH → 90

73 *What quality am I bringing?*

* * * * * * *

We lose a lot of the freshness of life by acting on auto-pilot, reacting to people and situations without even being aware of what we're bringing to the transaction. By asking, 'What quality am I bringing to this moment?' you immediately bring your attitude to light and, if necessary, you can choose an approach that's better for you and, hopefully, for everyone else too.

If you start asking the question above you may find, for instance, that you're bringing an unhelpful attitude of self-pity to an only slightly inconvenient piece of work. Once you see it, you can change it. The beauty of this exercise is that you don't have to spend ages looking for the answer. Just asking the question above is enough – it's that simple.

● *Practice*
Make a practice of asking yourself, 'What quality am I bringing to this moment?' Practise with something habitual, like a work meeting that happens several times a week or playing with a child or greeting someone in a local shop.

74 *Good news: it will never be perfect*

·······

Nothing will ever be perfect. Why is that good news? Because it means that, right now, you can drop the pursuit of perfection, which is a pursuit doomed to failure.

A common form of unhelpful thinking, identified in cognitive behavioural therapy (CBT), is to believe that if one thing is wrong, everything is wrong. If my date turns up ten minutes late, the evening is ruined, for instance. When you upset yourself over the fact that your life or even just your day is not exactly as you wanted it to be, you are failing to appreciate the miracle of some things going right for you in a universe in which you are, metaphorically, a grain of sand.

• *Practice*
Try resting for a little while in simple awareness of the moment without making any demands on that moment. Now try this with awareness of somebody who is emotionally close to you. Can you simply be aware of them without expectations or criticisms?

75 *We're storytellers*

· · · · · · ·

When somebody says something rude to you, do you repeat it to yourself in all sorts of different ways? Probably, because that's a human trait. Does it help? Almost certainly not.

We don't just tell a story: we add variations, going over and over different versions – the one in which you come out on top, the one in which they come out on top, the one in which the universe punishes the annoying person, etc. Has anyone in the history of the world felt better after doing this? I doubt it.

• *Practice*
When you find yourself complaining in your head for the umpteenth time about someone or something unpleasant, say, 'End of story' to remind yourself that many of the scenarios you are viewing right now are not real: they are just upsetting stories your brain is making up.

76 *Not all about me*

Mindfulness enhances relationships by making it easier for us to spot old patterns that harm communication. Today, try deliberately bringing a warm and interested awareness to your interactions with people who matter to you.

Mindfulness brings a greater sense of connection with others. Because we live in an interconnected world, that sense of connection is very useful. Moreover, belonging is a basic human psychological need, so the sense of connectedness helps fulfil that also. Your mindfulness won't directly change other people, but if you bring an awareness, appreciation and tolerance to the people who matter to you, they may respond in kind.

• *Practice*
If you're emotionally very close to someone and if you're in contact with them, try the experiment of communicating with them for twenty minutes without commenting on them in your head. Really give your attention to the person. You may find that this in itself improves the relationship (people love attention) and, who knows, you may even see them with new eyes.

77 Be sensational

· · · · · · ·

To come into the 'now' right now, notice your breathing, your hands, your feet – in other words, some aspect of your physical senses. Rest your attention on one of those senses for a little while, even half a minute.

To practise mindfulness you don't need a gong or a temple – you need your senses. Concepts such as the 'now' and the 'moment' are quite vague, so it isn't always helpful to say that mindfulness means coming into the 'now' or the 'moment'. If, instead, you think of mindfulness as deliberate awareness of what your senses are bringing you, it will be so much easier to do.

• Practice
Notice three sensations in a row; say, your breath, your posture, what you're hearing. Stay with each of these for a while. Your mind will wander – bring it back. All of this can take from a few seconds to a few minutes, depending on how much time you've got. As a frequent practice it can bring you into mindfulness several times a day.

78 *What do I feel?*

●●●●●●●

It can be better to ask 'What do I feel?' rather than 'How do I feel?' Give awareness to the physical sensation this brings up.* In time, the feeling will change.

Two things are happening when you get caught up in a feeling or mood, especially an unpleasant one. We could call the first 'Here is what I feel' and the second 'Here is what I'm telling myself about what I feel'. Sometimes it's the latter that prolongs the feeling. If you stay with awareness of the physical feeling, it will pass more quickly.

● *Practice*
When you find yourself in a sad or unpleasant mood, ask 'What do I feel?' The 'What' might refer to an overall feeling (I feel sad) or to a physical sensation (My stomach has a feeling of sadness). Allow yourself to have that physical sensation for a little while. Don't be afraid of it. It will soon pass.

*If you've had a traumatic experience, and if going into the physical sensation makes you feel uneasy, then use the other ideas in the book instead.

79 *Perfection's postponed –*
self-compassion's available

· · · · · · ·

The person towards whom you need to be self-compassionate is
the person you are right now. If you wait to achieve perfection,
you will wait for ever!

Among our oddest traits is the demand for perfection in our
lives – the perfect job, the perfect level of fitness, the perfect
partner, the perfect child. This would be amusing if we didn't
suffer because of it – feeling 'not good enough' or even angry at
ourselves and the world. Self-compassion, kindness towards the
imperfect person you already are, gives you a friend for life
(you) and will make it easier for others to like you too.

• *Practice*
When you catch yourself regretting your lack of perfection tell yourself
that 'good enough is good enough for me'. What's good enough will
vary from person to person and project to project. But never lose
sight of the philosophy that on a planet with more than 7 billion
competing human beings a 'good enough' life is a good life.

LABYRINTH → 2

80 *Noisy thoughts*

• • • • • • •

Some thoughts are helpful, but many are only noise. Today, whenever you realise you're lost in the noise, move awareness back to your breathing. Or else pay attention to what is going on in your surroundings.

You're not guaranteed a succession of noble or inspiring thoughts today. With luck, some will be gems, but lots will be as stimulating as the static from a badly tuned radio. Actually, that's ok – fun and frivolous thoughts can be relaxing – but when you realise your head is full of static that's neither fun nor helpful, switch to present-moment awareness. It's easier to do that if you are convinced of the value of mindfulness, which includes calm and a greater sense of positivity. And that's about returning your awareness to the ordinary moments of your day.

• *Practice*
Sit for a little while and observe your thoughts as though they flow past on a screen or like leaves on a stream. Notice the tiny gaps between thoughts. Give your attention to those gaps and watch them becoming longer. Rest in the gaps as the thoughts flow by.

LABYRINTH → 18

81 *It's out of control*

Fundamental to mindfulness is the understanding that much of what goes on in our personal world is outside our direct control. When we accept this, we worry less about perfection and predictability.

We've evolved as problem solvers. We tinker with things to fix them. That sometimes works, but we need to avoid the illusion that we should be able to control everything in our day. When we throw a ball in the air, gravity and the wind take over, often unhelpfully. Focus on what you can do (throw the ball, make the call, ask for help) and try to relax about the fact that the universe, in the form of people and events, might just go its own way.

● *Practice*
What do you plan to do today? How much is in your control? If it's just one–eighth, like the proportion of the iceberg that's said to be above the water, can you give more attention to that part than to the other seven–eighths?

82 *Compassionate body scan*

• • • • • • • •

Can you bring some compassion to your physical self? Your body has carried you around for years, often with little thanks. When doing a mindfulness exercise, such as the practice below, bring a sense of friendship and compassion to that body.

We cannot really separate our physical and emotional selves. And although we often practise mindfulness by becoming aware of aspects of our physical self, that's not helpful if we do so with disapproval, disappointment or annoyance. In doing the compassion scan below, we can bring a sense of friendship to our emotional self by bringing kindness to our physical self. Additionally, when paying attention to our breath or posture or walking, we can do so with a sense of kindness, liking and self-compassion.

• *Practice*
Bring awareness to the top of your head. Imagine self-compassion flowing into you from above. As you move your awareness down your body – trunk, tummy, legs, feet – imagine that self-compassion flowing alongside the awareness. When you finish, relax into that sense of self-compassion for a while.

83 *Knowing you*

• • • • • • •

As you practise mindfulness you become better at tuning in to how other people are feeling. In other words, you become more empathic. Self-talk, especially rerunning old judgements, gets in the way of this. So try to silence the mind for a few moments before you engage with others.

The insula – the part of the brain that helps us to sense how other people feel – is stimulated by mindfulness practice. We are social animals, so the greater empathy this gives us is a huge advantage as we navigate our way through family, college, work and play. The exercise below will make you more aware of your empathic relationship to others. Sometimes it may even give you a completely new perspective on them.

• *Practice*
Consider somebody you know well. Try to see them in your mind's eye. Now go silent in your mind. Try to get a sense of that person as someone for whom things go both well and badly, just like you. Then let the image fade.

LABYRINTH → 27

84 *Sit this one out*

Sometimes memories will start up in your head for no obvious reason. Perhaps a sound, or other event that you don't consciously notice, triggers them. If you woke up during the night to hear a band in the distance, you probably wouldn't get out of bed and dance. But what's the difference between that and uselessly going over and over some painful old memory? You're not obliged to engage with memories that do not serve you well.

● *Practice*
When you're tempted to go into an old, unhelpful memory, think of this urge as a band that has started playing in your mind and say, 'No thanks. I'm sitting this one out.' Then return to awareness of what you are doing.

85 *Mind your posture*

●●●●●●●

'Mind your posture' isn't an instruction to adopt the 'right' posture. It means coming into awareness of your posture (standing, walking, sitting, lying down or running) – a mindfulness exercise that goes back at least 2,000 years.

You may be using the right posture or the wrong one, but from the mindfulness point of view, all we are aiming for is awareness. It's often easier to be aware of posture than of anything else. If you like, you can combine it with awareness of your breathing. Awareness of posture generally relaxes us and if our posture is wrong, and if we know what is right, we generally adjust when we become aware.

● *Practice*
Notice your posture right now, whatever it may be. All you have to do is be conscious of it. Rest your mind in the awareness of the posture. Now change it slightly. If you are slumped in your chair, you might sit up, for instance. Now become mindful of that second posture for a while.

86 *Not happening*

· · · · · · ·

To weaken repetitive thoughts that may upset you, but don't help you, try using a phrase to stop them in their tracks and then get back to whatever you're doing. An example of such a phrase could be traditional, like 'this too will pass' or 'not happening'.

A disagreement with a colleague on Friday can bring a succession of distressing thoughts all weekend. Using a phrase like 'not happening' every time the thought comes to mind is a way of preventing it from taking over your whole weekend. It isn't so much that the thought goes away when you use the phrase – it's that it recedes into the background. If you don't feed it because you are getting on with something else, then the thought gradually goes away. And you get your weekend back.

• *Practice*
When repetitive thoughts come into your mind, especially if they make you stressed, try saying 'not happening' when you notice the thoughts and return your attention to the moment.

87 *Accept that*

· · · · · · ·

When you accept anything, from pain to a task you have to perform, you don't try to fool yourself into being delighted it's there. You accept that it exists, that you have to face it.

Acceptance is the other half of mindfulness. It isn't acquiescence, and it isn't agreeing that something should be so. It is about not resisting the fact that it is so, right now, at this moment. You may hope it will change, and even work to change it, but first you need to accept it is there. For instance, if you have a health problem, you need to accept that you have a problem before you can tackle it.

• *Practice*
Consider any problem you'd rather not have, but you've got it anyway. Begin by accepting the problem exists. Then ask what you can do about it. If the answer is nothing (if that health problem is chronic, for instance), then allow yourself to accept its presence in your life. If instead the answer is that you can – and should – do something about it (perhaps apologising for something hurtful you said), then accepting that this is so can make it easier to move forward and do what you should do.

88 *Sleep easy*

••••••••

If you tend to wake up in the night and lie there worrying, try doing a mindfulness practice instead.

Every night, people all over the world, including myself, use mindfulness to help them get back to sleep. My favourite is to focus on the breath in my nose followed, if I'm still awake, by a body scan. The more I've done this, the better it's worked. If you have trouble sleeping, join the rest of us mindful sleepers in bed!

• Practice

If you're awake in bed at night, do a slow body scan or bring aware-ness to the breath in your nose or do both, one after the other. For the body scan, move awareness slowly up your body from your feet to the top of your head. Name each part along the way: 'Toes, feet, calves, knees', etc.

89 Naikan: *give and take*

● ● ● ● ● ● ●

Acknowledging what we've received from and have given to other people is an effective way to experience a sense of gratitude. In the exercise below, you are encouraged to reflect on the specific details of what you have received and given.

In a Japanese practice called *Naikan*, you are invited to think of someone important to you and ask: 'What have I received from this person? What have I given this person? What difficulties have I caused this person?' The exercise can cut through resentments that may have soured a relationship from which you may have received more than you have acknowledged for some time. You can also feel good about acknowledging that you gave something to this person.

● *Practice*

Ask the three *Naikan* questions in relation to people who have been important to you at various times of your life up to the present. If you prefer, substitute 'What else have I received from this person?' for the third question. You could write the answers down as a list or journal entry instead of doing it all in your mind. Journalling can be a powerful way to sort out your thoughts and feelings about somebody or about a situation and it's one of my favourite daily activities.

90 *Dissonant chords*

......

In music, a dissonant chord strikes the wrong note. But in the context of the whole piece, the dissonance can highlight the overall harmony and deepen the listener's experience.

Dissatisfaction is an inescapable and everyday aspect of life – that's a key part of the mindfulness philosophy. What's crucial is to relate to life and its dissatisfactions in ways that make our experiences fulfilling despite them, and mindfulness helps us to do this. In mindfulness, we accept those dissonant chords as part of the overall music of life. You can apply the same approach to an event, a person or a day. All have their dissonant chords – but that doesn't stop them being worthwhile.

* *Practice*

Suppose you're feeling annoyed with someone you love. That's the dissonant chord. Think of the harmonies in the overall relationship. That's the context in which the dissonant chord occurs. It can help to remember this and to consider the harmony as well as the note that jars.

LABYRINTH → 76

91 *Wish well to your past self*

· · · · · · ·

We can all think of aspects of our past that we wish weren't there: what we have done or haven't done, what others have done or haven't done. To deliberately see our past self with compassion can lighten the burden of our personal history.

Perhaps we have failed to live up to our expectations or those of others. Perhaps others have hurt us. Perhaps things went wrong that left plans in ruins. But the memory of these experiences doesn't necessarily have to shape the rest of our lives. We can make choices starting from where we are now.

● *Practice*
Imagine a photograph of yourself at a point in the past. Look at the photograph and wish yourself well: 'Be happy, be safe, be well.' If you were not happy, safe or well, you could add the words: 'This is what I would have wished for you.' If you like, you can repeat this with an image from another part of your life.

92 *Juggling mindfulness*

. . . .

The image of mindfulness as requiring that you sit serenely in the lotus position is a cliché and is wrong. Mindfulness isn't about that – it's about directing your awareness to the present moment with acceptance of your experience in that moment.

What ordinary and absorbing activity could you use today to bring yourself into mindful awareness? Some star rugby players use Lego or colouring books to soothe their nerves between games. It's a mindful activity that works well for them. Elite sportspeople also use juggling – it's hard to think of a more mindful activity. So if being still with your hands in your lap is never going to work for you, try following their lead.

● *Practice*
Buy an adult colouring book and use it as a mindfulness practice. Alternatively, you could work on a jigsaw puzzle (be sure to focus on awareness, not on frustration!). Or use what's to hand: Solitaire, which you probably have on your phone or computer, can be a mindful activity.

LABYRINTH → 41

93 *How, not what*

Focusing on the process of carrying out a simple activity lessens the anxiety that can come with an excessive preoccupation with the outcome. With some of your activities today, try to keep returning awareness to what you are doing and how you are doing it rather than to what you hope (or fear) will happen in the end.

Of course, we need to know why we are doing something – what the goal of the activity is. In sports, for instance, performers know they want to win. However, freeing themselves from the anxiety that could trip them up means turning their attention to what they need to do right now, as opposed to the eventual hoped-for win. That's why mindfulness is increasingly adopted by athletes.

• *Practice*
Take a 'getting-nowhere' mindful walk. This could mean walking in a circle around a park or your garden and focusing on the experience, on the process, without being concerned with 'getting somewhere'.

LABYRINTH → 42

94 *Meet the critic*

How often do you make disparaging, i.e. hostile, remarks to yourself about yourself? The answer, I suspect, is quite often. But what sort of day would you have if you didn't? Why not find out?

Freud noted that each of us has a harsh critic in our head. He called it the superego. And we can't just blame our parents for it. Sometimes we ourselves create unrealistic expectations of perfection, which we then torment ourselves with. It's all irrational – but irrationality is part and parcel of the human condition, as you may have noticed. That's where mindfulness comes to our rescue: when we practise mindfulness we get better at spotting that the critic is in full spate. Once spotted, we can immediately step back from it, using the practice below.

• *Practice*
Use the phrase 'Hello critic, goodbye critic' whenever you notice that the old critic in your head has started attacking you again. If you genuinely need to change something, you'll still know that, but without beating yourself up.

95 *What are the facts?*

•••••••

Your brain interprets what's going on. Sometimes its interpretations add unhelpful negativity to your day. Could you be mindful today about what 'spin' your mind is putting on events and feelings and take a mental step back from its exaggerated stories?

The mind weaves theories about what's happening even in the absence of facts: 'My team leader hasn't got back to me about that idea I emailed her [fact]. She must hate it so much she can't be bothered to talk to me about it [story].' Worse, you may now react to your story by resenting her: 'Who does she think she is anyway?' The way to avoid this pointless sequence is to seek facts: ask her.

• *Practice*
Imagine that one side of your brain deals in facts and the other side in stories and interpretations about these facts. When you find your-self in a loop of exaggerated stories about what's going on, ask, 'And what are the facts?' to get a less stressful perspective. You could even turn this exercise into a game with a friend to whom you would explain your emotional issue and they would reply again and again, 'And what are the facts?' (until you tell them to stop). Similarly, you could do this for your friend.

96 *A boulder on the path*

• • • • • • •

If you find a large boulder blocking your path, you could stand staring at it or you could walk around it and go on. Do you have any metaphorical boulders in your path that it would be ok to bypass?

It's not always that simple, I know. Sometimes you can't just walk away. Other alternatives to being stopped in your tracks are to seek advice or support. Each of these options – which, if you're really stuck, might be the ones you've been ignoring – is more effective than standing there generating fears or resentments in your head. But you can't move all obstacles (a bullying boss, for example), in which case moving on might be the healthiest choice.

• *Practice*
Look at an obstacle you face. Do you need to remove it? Could you walk around it and continue on your path? If not, could you look at it from another angle? Whose opinion do you respect? What would they do? Who could you ask for help?

LABYRINTH → 4

97 *Mindful hands*

· · · · · · ·

Become aware of how your hands feel right now and what they are doing. Can you feel the energy in them? Notice the touch of a cup or of fabric, of a piece of wood, stone or paper. This is mindfulness, but with touch rather than breath. You might prefer it if you dislike awareness of your breathing.

To comfort somebody or to show that you are there for them you might touch or hold their hand. Hands are important to us humans, emotionally as well as practically. It's a pity we forget them so often. Practising awareness of touch reminds us that a moment isn't just an intellectual concept. It's also a touch, a voice, a scent, a breeze on your face.

• Practice

In your mind's eye, move your awareness up and down the fingers of each hand. If you prefer, run the index finger of one hand along each finger of the other hand and then swap around. Do it slowly, though, and really experience it.

LABYRINTH → 16

98 *One dog multiplied*

. . . .

Mindfulness isn't about never being afraid, but when we are mindful we don't multiply our fears. So if you're fearful of something today, try to focus on what's essential and real, and don't indulge the sensationalised versions your mind scares you with.

Suppose you are out walking and a dog stands in your path. Suppose you don't like dogs. Your mind can exaggerate the experience ('What if he wants to bite me? What if he has rabies?'), so that the dog might as well be three times bigger and fierce enough for three dogs. Return to dealing with the actual dog (who hopefully just wants to sniff out who you are) – it's much easier.

● *Practice*
Looking at anything you feel anxious about, draw an imaginary line: on the left, put the simplest true statement you can make (a dog is on the path); on the right, put exaggerations and speculations (maybe he's an angry guard dog, maybe there's a gang of them). Focus on the left-hand column.

99 *The smallest thing*

• • • • • • •

An effective way to practise mindfulness is to look for the smallest item or experience you could be aware of. Most of us, after all, don't have a mountain or ocean to practise on (but if you do, try a pebble or a shell).

Mindfulness is almost always about detail. Your breath is one tiny detail in the whole universe. So is the feeling of your feet against the soles of your shoes. So is the taste of your food. Right now, I'm aware of the sound of my fingers on the keyboard as I write this. If I tried to be aware of the whole process of writing it wouldn't work – my mind would quickly slip away down some side road. For mindfulness practice, detail is your friend.

• Practice
If you're walking in a park or in your own garden, could you notice one flower at a time as a mindfulness practice? Perhaps you could make a mental list of details to regularly look out for? This would help to structure your garden walk, so that your mind doesn't just wander off down a tangled path of rumination which means repeating anxious, sad or angry thoughts over and over again. You could also use the mindful-walk instructions that you will find in the Appendix.

LABYRINTH → 92

100 *Simple moments*

· · · · · · ·

We seem to have lost patience with simple moments. We escape from them as quickly as we can, usually into a smartphone. Reverse the direction now and then: escape from the phone into the simple moments.

Returning to simple moments is a really good way to build our capacity for mindful awareness. That, in turn, builds our capacity for calm. Remember: simple moments are what your life is made up of (unless you're a superhero). They are also what those who want to sell you their latest gadgets try to divert you from. So coming back into a simple moment is also an act of self-assertiveness and autonomy.

• *Practice*
In situations where you might be tempted to seek distraction (on the train, at your desk), take a few moments to rest your attention on something simple. This could be as uncomplicated as the steam rising from a cup of coffee. In this way, you have trained yourself to be more aware, more mindful, less distractible.

Themed guide

Here you will find suggested practices to look at, listed by theme. These can be helpful when you have a particular issue or concern:

Pressure at work

Relationships

Anxiety

Feeling low

Anger

Appendix:

A mindful walk in seven stages

One easy and effective way to make mindfulness part of your day is to take a mindful walk in which you bring yourself through a number of stages that reflect various aspects of the practice.

This is easier than it might sound, as you'll see from the instructions below. I should add that you could do this without actually going on a walk. I have even taken a mindful walk in my mind in bed during the night! The advantage of an actual mindful walk, however, is that eventually it will remind you to be mindful whenever you are out walking.

You will find seven instructions below. At the end of each stage is a symbol. The purpose of the symbol is to give you an easy visual way to remember the stages of the walk. So, for instance, the sun (stage 1) represents the light of awareness, which helps you to remember the first stage of bringing your attention to whatever you are aware of right now in your vicinity. Each symbol leads on from the previous one and I still find this a very useful way to remember all the stages of the walk.

When a stage or an example is related to one of the 100 ideas in this book, I have given the number representing that idea in brackets.

Here, then, are the stages:

1 • *Ask: what five things am I aware of right now?*
This means what am I aware of in my vicinity? This could be people, traffic, trees, sounds, the feeling of my feet against the ground, the smell of flowers or shrubs. Or I could be aware of my own breathing, my posture, maybe a physical feeling I have (21).

SYMBOL: *the sun – light of awareness*

2 • *What five things do I accept right now?*

This could mean accepting how I feel, or something that is happening in my world or in somebody else's. It could mean accepting that I have to perform some unpleasant task later today, or I could just be accepting the weather (87).

SYMBOL: *a bowl accepting the light from the sun and holding the light in acceptance*

3 • *Bring awareness to my breath.*

This means observing a number of in-breaths and out-breaths. For me, this usually means five in-breaths and out-breaths. But the number isn't really all that important; it could be fewer or more (4).

SYMBOL: *imagine the light being drawn up out of the bowl by your breath*

4 • *Say an affirmation.*

This means repeating an affirmation that you find helpful a few times. It helps to turn your thoughts in a more useful direction. You can develop your own affirmations. Here are a few that I use: my happiness does not depend on this (51); let it be (17); if I can find happiness in this, I am liberated (8); my life is not a game of chess – in other words, I don't have to spend every moment problem-solving (2).

SYMBOL: *the word 'affirmation' appears in the light that your breath drew out of the bowl*

5 • *What's positive?*

List five things that are positive. This is just to help turn your mind in a lighter direction. It also helps you to avoid getting caught in a harmful loop of thoughts in which you attack yourself or other people or life in general over and over (32). The things that are positive don't have to be about the main issue that is on your mind today. They could be that the sky is blue, that somebody you know is happy, that you're looking forward to tomorrow, that you are able to make the choice to go on a walk like this (63) and that you enjoy the breeze on your face.

SYMBOL: *the light becomes a circle in the sky; in other words, it becomes the sun again, representing what's positive*

6 • *Remember self-compassion.*
This means reminding yourself that you will still be your own true friend at the end of the day, whatever may happen. Or it could be at the end of a piece of work you're doing, or of a social event you're unsure about (3).

SYMBOL: *the sun becomes a heart*

7 • *Remember courage.*
This means connecting with your own power. It means knowing what your intentions are and doing what needs to be done, even if you feel nervous about it (40).

SYMBOL: *the heart becomes a shield that could be held by a warrior – male or female, as you wish*

To help you remember the stages above with ease, just take a moment to run through the visual symbols in your head once or twice now:

The sun, light of awareness, is held in a bowl of acceptance, the light is drawn up by your breath, the word 'affirmation' appears in the light, the light becomes a sun again for the positive aspects of your day or your life, the sun takes the shape of a heart for self-compassion and the heart becomes a shield for courage. A useful trick for remembering a sequence like this is to repeat it to yourself backwards a couple of times.

Helpful resources

- **Books**

Mindfulness on the Go: Peace in your pocket (Padraig O'Morain)
If you want to know more about mindfulness, you will find
what you need here presented in an accessible way with lots of
exercises.

Mindfulness for Worriers: Overcome everyday stress and anxiety
(Padraig O'Morain)
This book is especially for those (probably all of us) who make
stress and anxiety worse than they need to be.

*Kindfulness: Be a true friend to yourself – with mindful self-
compassion* (Padraig O'Morain)
Learn to be your own friend in all life's situations.

Light Mind: Mindfulness for daily living (Padraig O'Morain)
A comprehensive introduction to mindfulness and to how to
apply it.

*Don't Sweat the Small Stuff . . . and It's All Small Stuff:
Simple ways to keep the little things from taking over your
life* (Richard Carlson)
This is not overtly a mindfulness book, but it is based solidly on
mindfulness principles. One to dip into.

*Wherever You Go, There You Are: Mindfulness meditation for
everyday life* (Jon Kabat-Zinn)
Brief reflections from the major figure in the popularisation of
mindfulness in recent decades.

- *Websites*

padraigomorain.com
Lots of free mindfulness resources and ideas including audios.

todoinstitute.org
Read about simple and effective mindfulness practices from Japanese psychology.

everyday-mindfulness.org
Everyday Mindfulness is all about applying mindfulness to your everyday life.

www.freemindfulness.org
Lots of free audios (including some by myself) and other resources too.

wildmind.org
Wildmind is a very accessible website for those who are interested in Buddhist meditation.

- *Newsletters*

The Daily Bell
Thousands of people all over the world receive my free, daily mindfulness email. Many say they find it invaluable (subscribe at www.padraigomorain.com).

Padraig O'Morain's Mindfulness Newsletter
This free newsletter, issued by email at irregular intervals, includes brief articles on mindfulness, as well as links to resources.

- ### *Other resources*

Courses
I present a variety of mindfulness courses both online and at venues in Ireland and the UK. To keep in touch with what's on, where and when, subscribe to my Daily Bell mindfulness reminder.

Insight Timer
A popular and useful app for iPhone, iPad and Android.

Facebook
My Facebook mindfulness page is at: facebook.com/PadraigOMorainMindfulness

My Facebook Mindfulness Forum, on which members share experiences about mindfulness as well as mindfulness resources, is at: facebook.com/groups/BetterMindful

Acknowledgements

My sister, Maria Flynn, advised me some years ago to make my mindfulness courses accessible to people who did not already practise meditation. I took her advice and this book is one of the many outcomes of following that path. I am grateful to her, and also to my publisher, Liz Gough, and to Holly Whitaker, both of Yellow Kite Books, to my editor Anne Newman, to May van Millingen for the illustrations and to my agent, Susan Feldstein. My family is an unfailing source of support.

You may also enjoy reading
Padraig O'Morain's other books:

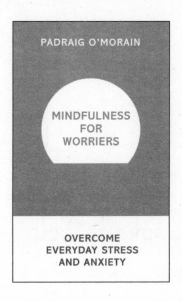

yellow
kite

books to help you live a good life

Join the conversation and tell
us how you live a #goodlife

🐦 @yellowkitebooks
f YellowKiteBooks
📌 Yellow Kite Books
📷 YellowKiteBooks